Contents

How well do you know your e-tiquette?

How often do you feel overcome by the amount of messages in your inbox?
a) Never   b) Sometimes   c) Constantly

To what extent is your working life improved by e-mail?
a) Immeasurably   b) Very much   c) Not at all

How often do you send e-mails which you later regret?
a) Rarely   b) Sometimes   c) Regularly

How many personal e-mails do you receive each day?
a) Less than 10   b) 11–20   c) Over 20

How regularly do you gossip or make personal comments over e-mail?
a) Very rarely   b) Sometimes   c) Very regularly

How aware are you of the rules your organisation applies to e-mailing?
a) Very   b) Fairly   c) Not at all

How many different uses do you put e-mails to, aside from basic e-mailing (for example, group e-mails, newsletters, interest groups, sales, marketing etc)?
a) Over 5   b) 2–5   c) None

How soon after receiving an e-mail do you reply?
a) It depends on the importance of the message
b) Fairly soon, especially for the important ones
c) Immediately

How many messages are usually in your inbox?
a) Under 50   b) 50–150   c) Don't have a clue!

How often do you 'prune' your inbox by filing some messages and deleting others?
a) Every day
b) Every couple of months
c) When my mailbox crashes and I'm told to!

What do you usually write in the subject line?
a) There is no 'usual' — I write whatever's relevant
b) Greetings or Hello!
c) I usually leave it blank

a = 1, b = 2, and c = 3.
Now add up your scores.

Chapter **1** explains how you can make the most of your e-mail tools, so should be useful for everyone.

- **11–17:** You appear to be adept at e-mailing, but there is always room for improvement. Chapter **4** will help you develop your e-mail negotiation skills. Beware of relying on e-mail too heavily—sometimes there are better alternatives. Read chapter **6** for advice on combining e-mail with other forms of communication.
- **18–26:** You use e-mails fairly comfortably, but be wary of becoming overconfident. Some companies monitor e-mails, so read chapter **8** for advice on using e-mail responsibly. Chapter **5** should help you out if you encounter a tricky e-mail situation.
- **26–36:** You seem to let e-mails get the better of you. First, recover control of your inbox by following the advice in chapter **2**. Then read chapter **3** and improve your e-mail style; once your confidence increases, you will be able to discover the multiple uses of e-mail—chapter **7** offers some ideas.

Making the most of e-mail

In 2003, 35 billion e-mails were sent every day and by 2006 that figure is forecast to rise to more than 65 billion. It's a massive understatement to say that e-mail is an essential part of the working day—in many ways, it has replaced the telephone or face-to-face meetings as the most popular way to exchange information.

Some commentators believe that people at work don't really understand the true potential of e-mail, though. There is little formal training and the result is often poor communication, time-wasting, and frustration at the 'tyranny' of e-mail. Leave the office for a day and you could face over 50 e-mails on your return. When you receive a new message, what should you do— stop everything and reply immediately? And suppose you make a careless remark to a colleague via e-mail—could you face disciplinary procedures or legal action?

These downsides do exist, but e-mail has a positive role to play in making it easier to communicate with colleagues, customers, or suppliers. It speeds up the transmission of important information and helps people to work together more effectively.

This chapter sets out to help you get the most from e-mail while you're at work.

Step one: Understand what e-mail is

E-mail—electronic mail—is a method of sending messages or other information from one computer to another. An e-mail can consist of a short message, similar in content to an internal memo or fax, or it can be a more substantial document, such as a report or a presentation.

Simple e-mail can be used to send short messages or make arrangements, such as 'Can you make a meeting at 10.00?' Longer e-mails take the place of memos or faxes and can be the equivalent of one or more pages in length. They can also include longer documents, photographs, audio files, or video clips that are sent with the message and are called attachments.

E-mails can be sent to recipients within a single organisation over a network, or to recipients anywhere in the world via the Internet. Depending on the speed of the network or Internet connection, an e-mail can reach recipients in seconds, wherever they're located.

E-mail has revolutionised the way many of us work and has made global communications a reality, 24 hours a day. It means you can exchange information with colleagues, customers, and suppliers quickly and easily, whatever the time and wherever you are.

Step two: Use e-mail to improve internal communications

Wherever you work, e-mail is a great way to maintain effective contact with colleagues and save yourself time (although it can be over-used). Rather than try to reach someone by phone, pop along to their office, or set up a meeting, it's quicker and easier to send an informative e-mail. It's also an excellent way to communicate discreetly with colleagues, and causes least disruption. E-mail is ideal if you want to:

- let the recipient have some information
- confirm an arrangement
- give detailed instructions
- make a request
- provide news that has value

Compare the time it takes to do that by e-mail with the time you might spend on redialling engaged extensions, sharing initial pleasantries on the phone, or sitting through delays in meetings. E-mail becomes less effective (and at times unwieldy) if you need to have a detailed discussion, but it can be a useful starting point.

It's also a quick and easy way for companies to let all employees know about a new development or important announcement. One message to all employees can take just minutes to create and distribute.

Step three: Work more effectively with other people

If you're part of a team working together on a particular project or activity, e-mail is a very effective method of collaborating. In fact, this was one of e-mail's biggest applications when it first became common in business.

✔ Use e-mail to keep every member up to date with relevant developments. Project documents can be shared quickly and easily. E-mail ensures that everyone has the same information and this can reduce the time spent on progress meetings. It can also be used to make team members aware of any issues that need to be resolved quickly.

TOP TIP
If you work with colleagues in different locations, you can eliminate unnecessary travelling and reach decisions quickly by using e-mail to exchange information.

Step four: Maintain better contact with customers

If your work is related to sales or customer service, e-mail is an ideal way to maintain regular contact with customers and to communicate quickly about urgent issues.

✔ You can use e-mail to advise customers of a variety of news, including:

- new product developments
- delivery dates
- price changes
- special offers

✔ E-mail can reduce the time it takes to resolve queries or deal with incoming correspondence. Send an initial e-mail by return to show the customer that you've received their query and are working on it. Many companies set targets for responding to customer letters or e-mails (for example, 'we aim to reply to all queries within three working days'). As soon as you have the answer, you can reply in full, with no postal delays to worry about.

Step five: Keep personal e-mail under control

E-mail's speed and simplicity mean that employees find it useful for personal communication as well as business use. E-mails used to confirm social arrangements, order personal goods and services, or just exchange news may seem harmless. However, the growing volume of e-mail has resulted in many organisations now attempting to control and restrict personal use in order to keep the systems clear for business communications. For example, some local government authorities have introduced 'e-mail free days', while many companies publish strict guidelines on personal use of e-mail. You may also find that your company monitors e-mails as part of its Internet security programme. See chapter 8 for more information on this thorny issue.

TOP TIP
Be careful what you say in personal e-mails—they can have the same legal status as a letter. Careless gossip could be misunderstood and could get you in trouble.

Step six: Understand the rules

This book covers the key issues of e-mail etiquette, explaining what is acceptable in terms of content, punctuation, spelling, and tone of voice. It also describes what to do if things go wrong, for example if you reply in haste, send an incorrect message by mistake, or if you encounter rudeness in an e-mail.

Be aware, though, that individual organisations may also have specific regulations for the use of e-mail.

✔ Check with someone on your IT helpdesk to see if your organisation has its own guidelines on what is acceptable in e-mails. There may be rules about how long you need to retain e-mails for legal reasons and guidelines on personal use of e-mail.

Common mistakes

✗ You don't take e-mail seriously

E-mail is a powerful form of communication and is easy to use. Try not to let this aspect of it transfer to the messages you write, though, and remember that it's important to write business e-mails with the same degree of care that you would use in composing a letter.

✗ You overuse it

You can write a short e-mail very quickly and be confident that it will reach the recipient in minutes or, in some cases, seconds. Because of that, it's tempting to send more e-mails than you really need to, or resort to it when other methods of communication would be more appropriate. Remember that in some circumstances, such as complicated negotiations or detailed decision-making, it's more efficient to phone someone or meet face to face.

STEPS TO SUCCESS

✔ Understand when and why e-mail should be used and recognise when it isn't appropriate.

✔ If you're not convinced of the benefits of e-mail, think about how you can expand your communications by using it: there are no time or geographical boundaries to e-mail.

✔ Use e-mail to communicate more effectively with people inside your own organisation and to work more effectively with other people.

✔ Strengthen your links to customers with well-written and useful messages.

✔ Don't make excessive use of e-mail for personal reasons.

✔ Make sure you understand your company's policy on e-mail use in general and personal e-mails in particular.

Useful links

'A Beginner's Guide to Effective Email', webfoot.com:
www.webfoot.com/advice/email.top.html
Career Planning:
www.careerplanning.about.com
Netiquette home page:
www.albion.com/netiquette
Office Survival, CC Consulting:
www.crazycolour.com/os/hb06-01.shtml

Keeping on top of e-mail

E-mail has completely changed the way we work today. It offers many benefits and, if used well, can be an excellent tool for improving your own efficiency. Managed badly, though, e-mail can be a waste of valuable time. Statistics indicate that office workers need to wade through an average of more than 30 e-mails a day, while managers or people working on collaborative projects could be dealing with a much higher figure.

This chapter sets out steps to help you manage the time you spend dealing with e-mail so that you can get on with other tasks. It offers help on prioritising those incoming messages and deciding how quickly you need to respond. It tells you how to file e-mail according to its value or function and encourages you to clear your inbox regularly.

Despite your best efforts, unsolicited e-mail or spam can clutter up the most organised inbox and can even bring work to a standstill by infecting your computer system with viruses, so this section gives guidance on ways of protecting yourself. It also suggests alternatives to e-mail communication that offer the same benefits of speed, convenience, and effectiveness.

Step one: Prioritise incoming messages

If you're regularly faced with a large volume of incoming messages, you need to prioritise your inbox—identify which e-mails are really important.

✔ Check the names of the senders. Were you expecting or hoping to hear from them? How quickly do you need to deal with particular individuals?

✔ Check the subject. Is it an urgent issue or just information? Is it about an issue that falls within your sphere or responsibility, or is it something that should just be forwarded to someone else?

✔ Check the priority given by the senders. Do they really mean it's urgent? Remember that some people have a tendency to mark all of their messages 'important', even if they're anything but.

✔ Is it obvious spam? Does it look like a virus because it has an attachment and comes from an unknown sender? Can it be deleted without reading?

✔ Check when the message was sent. Has it been in your inbox a long time?

An initial scan like this can help you identify the e-mails that need your immediate attention. The others can be kept for reading at a more convenient time.

Step two: Reply in stages

Because e-mail is an 'instant' medium, it can be tempting to reply immediately but that might not always be necessary. You can reply in stages, with a brief acknowledgement and a more detailed follow-up. If you do this, give the recipient an indication of when you'll be able to get back to him or her and try to keep to this deadline wherever possible.

✔ If the e-mail simply requires a brief, one-line answer then by all means reply immediately. For example, if all you need to say is, 'Yes, I can make the 10.00 meeting', or 'Thanks, that's just the information I needed', do it.

✔ If you're unable to reply there and then or choose not to, let the sender know that you've received the message and that you'll be in touch as soon as possible. This is a polite and useful method of dealing with an e-mail query when:

- you need to get further information before replying in full
- it relates to a relatively complex issue so you need time to consider your response, rather than giving a rushed answer
- you're angry, upset, frustrated, or confused about a message you've received and need a 'cooling-off' period before you make a considered response

TOP TIP

Taking a staged approach is a useful strategy that allows you to maintain contact while not interrupting other work that may be more important. It also gives you a bit of breathing space if you're feeling under pressure or worried about the issue under discussion.

Step three: Set specific times for dealing with incoming e-mail

Good time management is essential in all areas of your life and e-mail is no exception. If you're completely overwhelmed by the volume of messages in your inbox, dedicate a certain amount of time each day to sorting it out.

✔ If you don't work in a traditional office setting you may have 'dial-up' e-mail where you contact a service provider to check your inbox. Set a pattern for dialling-in that fits in well with the type of work you do and the amount of e-mails you expect, and stick to it.

✔ If you have a broadband connection that is 'always on', your computer will let you know when you receive a new message. Think about whether to review the new messages immediately or wait till a pre-determined time. For example, if you have preferred working patterns or core working hours—times when you need to be

available for contact with overseas clients, for example—
you may decide to dedicate a certain portion of the day
to dealing with your e-mail.

TOP TIP

**If you spend a lot of time in meetings, you may
find that you have short spells between
meetings (say 10 or 15 minutes) that
would otherwise be wasted time. Use
these breaks to catch up with your
e-mail so that you don't have a flood of
them waiting for you at the end of the day.**

Step four: Use a filing system to manage your messages

What do you do with incoming messages once you've read
them? If the information is important, you may want to keep
it for future reference. However, hoarding all your messages
in no particular order will not only slow you down when you
are looking for information, but may also make your
computer system unwieldy and likely to crash.

✔ Check whether your company has a policy for retaining
and storing e-mails. Archiving may be essential for legal
reasons and if there is a policy in place, you must comply
with it. Your company may have a central facility for
storing or accessing archived e-mails so investigate

with your computer officer or helpdesk, if you have one. You'll be making their lives easier as well!

✔ If you have a lot of important information you need to hang on to (deals done over e-mail for example, or sign-offs from partners), create your own filing system. For example, you could sort messages into folders arranged by:

- customer or supplier name
- project name
- date of receipt
- research topic

✔ Use subfolders: for example, for each project it may be useful to subdivide everything into monthly or yearly folders. This will also make it easier to see what should be archived and when.

TOP TIP

To save space in your inbox, you might want to copy important e-mails relating to a specific project or programme into other applications. For example, you could create a Word document called 'project communications', in which all relevant e-mails or messages are held centrally. Everyone will then be able to access the information if you are away for any reason and you will all be able to find what you need quickly.

Step five: Practise good housekeeping

If you don't file your incoming messages as described in Step four, make sure you comb through your inbox regularly. If your inbox is chock-full with every message you've received during the course of a working week, a simple search for an important message could take an awful lot of time.

TOP TIP
Unless you need to keep messages for legal reasons, it's generally good practice to delete them regularly. Regular 'pruning' will help you keep on top of things. To help you do this, some e-mail applications offer an option that asks you if want to empty your deleted items folder every time you exit the application. This useful option will ease you into good e-mail management practice.

✔ Set time limits for keeping messages in your inbox.

✔ File or archive any messages that you need to keep.

✔ Make sure that you've replied if a response was necessary.

✔ Keep any valuable information, such as contact names or phone numbers.

✔ Send unwanted messages to the 'deleted messages' section of your e-mail system, but check again before you finally clear that section.

Step six: Make arrangements for e-mails when you're away

Opening your inbox after a holiday or a few days away can be an intimidating experience. 'You have 90 new messages'—where do you begin? Step one, 'Prioritise incoming messages', is a good starting point, but a few minutes spent making arrangements before you leave the office will save you a lot of time on your return.

✔ Leave an 'out of office reply' on your system. This responds automatically to incoming e-mails, telling the sender that you are away and will deal with the message on your return. It won't stop the first message from a particular sender, but it may prevent further material or messages from the same person asking why you haven't replied.

✔ As part of your 'out of office reply', state when you are back in the office so that your correspondent has a rough idea of how long you'll be away. If you are expecting a lot of messages or are at a crucial stage in a big project, ask one of your colleagues if you can nominate them to be an alternative point of contact during your absence, and if your colleague agrees,

give his or her e-mail and telephone number in your
'out of office reply'.

✔ Alternatively, ask a colleague to check your inbox
regularly for particular types of message and either
acknowledge them or deal with the issue, if possible.
This will make sure that urgent items receive the right
level of attention.

Step seven: Offer alternatives to e-mail

Although e-mail is one of the most popular and convenient
ways of communicating quickly, there are practical and
effective alternatives:

■ instant messaging, which allows short messages to be
communicated between connected computers on a
network. This is ideal for brief communications, such as
'meeting changed to 11.00', or 'send me the latest sales
figures'.
■ voicemail, which again allows the caller to leave
messages that you can respond to when you're
ready
■ teleconferencing, where a number of people can join
in a telephone discussion and make decisions without
long e-mail chains
■ introduction of informal meeting areas which promote
real collaboration

A good deal of e-mail communication comes from external sources, but think about how many e-mails you send each day to your colleagues in the office, or receive from them. Are they all absolutely necessary? If not, why not take the initiative and ask whoever is responsible for company-wide e-mail management to instigate some basic rules that will cut down on internal e-mails? The policies could cover:

- mass copies of e-mail to recipients who don't really need it (for example, sending an e-mail about a project to everyone in the business when only a small group of people need to be kept informed)
- personal e-mail
- limits on the 'thread' of a discussion which covers every point made by every recipient

Step eight: Protect against spam

Spam or unwanted e-mail, like the unsolicited direct mail that comes through your letterbox, is a tremendous waste of time and can clog up your e-mail system.

It's a real and growing problem for businesses in the United Kingdom: in December 2003, the Institute for Enterprise and Innovation at the University of Nottingham found that UK office workers spent up to an hour per day deleting spam from their inboxes. That hour could be very well spent tackling other items on your to-do list, so think about the following ways to limit or prevent spam:

✔ Use a filter supplied by your Internet service provider. This blocks e-mails that contain certain terms or other attributes that identify the message as potential spam.

✔ If it's practical, set rules for your incoming e-mail. Some rules block all incoming e-mail except messages from addresses you've nominated. This is helpful to a certain degree, but can cause problems for new legitimate contacts or organisations that have changed their addresses.

✔ Unsubscribe to any services or newsletters that that you do not wish to receive. The incoming e-mail should provide you with details of how to do this.

✔ Use a separate e-mail address for newsgroups as spammers use these addresses for their mailing lists.

✔ Do not give permission for your e-mail address to be passed on to other parties when you subscribe to or register for a new service. At some stage in the registration or subscription process, you should be asked whether or not you give permission for this to happen, normally in the form of a short statement plus a preference box that you need to tick or untick. Read any such requests very carefully.

✔ As a last resort, change your e-mail address. It might take less time to send a new e-mail address to everyone on your contact list than it does to delete your daily spam load.

TOP TIP

Not only does spam clog up your inbox,
but it can pass on viruses that may spread
throughout your computer system. You
should immediately delete any suspicious
e-mails and then empty your 'deleted items'
folder. Most companies will have invested
in the most up-to-date anti-virus software
they can afford, but if you work from home
or are self-employed, it's up to you to
make sure your machine is virus-free.
Scan your computer regularly for viruses
and make sure you have the relevant
software and security patches. The links
at the end of the chapter will help you
find out more about this.

Common mistakes

✗ **Reacting immediately to every e-mail**
Like a ringing telephone, it can be hard to ignore a new incoming message. It takes discipline to wait for a convenient moment or scan the message and reply later, but once you've decided on a new approach to dealing with e-mail, stick to it.

✗ **Not clearing your inbox regularly**
The list of incoming messages can very quickly grow to unmanageable proportions. Clear the inbox regularly or

develop a filing system that allows you to respond appropriately and retain useful information.

✗ Not protecting against spam

Spam doesn't just waste your time and fill up your inbox, it can also introduce harmful viruses into your computer or your company network. Make sure you are protected against unwanted e-mail and seek advice from your computer helpdesk team or Internet service provider if you have any concerns.

STEPS TO SUCCESS

✔ Prioritise your incoming messages—not every e-mail is urgent or important.

✔ Reply when you are ready—an instant medium doesn't require an instant response.

✔ Choose a convenient time to deal with non-urgent e-mail.

✔ Develop a filing system that allows you to retain and use valuable information.

✔ Clear your inbox regularly to prevent your system from becoming unmanageable.

✔ Make arrangements to deal with e-mail when you're away from the office so that you don't return to a mountain of messages.

✔ Consider alternatives to e-mail such as instant messaging, voicemail, or face-to-face contact.

✔ Protect yourself against spam by using filters or imposing rules on incoming mail.

Useful links

BBC Webwise:
www.bbc.co.uk/webwise/askbruce/articles/email/index.shtml
McAfee antivirus software:
www.mcafee.com
Norton antivirus software:
www.norton.com

Writing great e-mails

Although e-mail is a widely-used medium, many people do not know how to use it well. As it's an 'instant' way of getting in touch with others, it's easy to overlook the basics of business correspondence such as spelling, grammar, and punctuation in e-mails, but it's important that you maintain high standards however you communicate with others.

The style you use for a message will clearly depend on the recipient, but take time in judging what you're writing to whom so that your company's image or reputation is always enhanced, never diminished.

Every e-mail should have a clearly identified subject so that the recipient can quickly decide how important the message is. Although you can use terms such as 'urgent' or 'high priority' to alert the recipient, try to use them only when absolutely necessary as otherwise the impact will be lessened.

This chapter offers more advice on the essentials of writing effective e-mails, and also includes help on using attachments and signatures.

Step one: Clearly identify the subject of the e-mail

As e-mail grows in popularity, people in business receive a high volume of messages each day. To deal with this potential flood, they have to prioritise and decide what is important. Make sure, then, that every e-mail you send has a clearly-identified subject.

Most popular e-mail packages include a subject line, so use this to state as concisely as possible what your e-mail is about. Examples include:

- new date for meeting
- price changes on the ABC range
- sales monthly report
- order for Customer XYZ—delivery status
- new managing director appointed

These are brief and to the point but they indicate clearly what the e-mail is about.

TOP TIP

Even if you're on reasonably friendly terms with the recipient, if you're writing a *business* e-mail, try to avoid using 'Hello' in the subject line. It annoys some people and they may even be put off reading the message.

✔ Some e-mails cover a subject that changes over a period of time, such as the content of a new brochure or the status of a project. To help everyone keep track of the changes and to make sure they read the latest version of information, add a date or version number to the title. For example:

- new brochure copy—draft 4
- project status—July
- revised personnel guidelines—effective December

Step two: Be as concise as possible

An e-mail is, first and foremost, a *short* form of communication. It should be brief and to the point and the recipient should be able to understand the main points of your message in the first few lines.

✔ As most e-mails will be read on a small computer screen, it can be difficult and inconvenient to follow long passages of text. If you need to go into more detail, send a document as a separate attachment or tell the recipient to contact you for more information.

✔ If you need to go into some detail and sending an attachment isn't possible, break your message into small 'chunks' with a heading before each new section. This will make long passages of information easier to read and understand on screen and your correspondents will be able to pick out the most relevant information for them.

Example of clear e-mail structure

Let's say you're thinking of creating a new project and would like your correspondent to be a contributor. To save them trawling through a dense paragraph, you could give a brief overview of the project and then highlight key points:

Your role
To overhaul our annual product catalogue, liaising with teams in-house on content and delivering final files to the printer.

Budget
£800.00 (40 hours at £20.00 per hour).

Deadline
Final files delivered no later than 30 September.

Step three: Check your spelling and punctuation

An e-mail is a form of business correspondence that has the same status as letters and other printed material. In the hands of a customer, it reflects on the image of the company, so a message riddled with spelling mistakes

and bad grammar isn't going to show you in your
best light.

TOP TIP

**The popularity of text messages and text
message speak is beginning to creep
over into e-mail. While most people will
understand what you mean if you send
them a message along the lines of 'C U
at 10' or 'mtg off', it's best not to include
this type of abbreviation in messages
to external clients or contacts. Use
full correct spelling, even if this
takes a little longer.**

✔ Take a few minutes to check your message for
mistakes and sense before you send it. Many popular
e-mail programs include spellcheckers to help you do
this, but if your system doesn't have one, you could
prepare your message in a word processing program,
check it, and then copy the final version into your
e-mail.

✔ Remember to use upper and lower case letters in your
messages to business contacts. Writing a message
completely in lower case gives an impression of
something written in haste. Your correspondent might
think that you just couldn't be bothered to spend any
time on it (and, by extension, them). Writing it all in upper
case may look as if you're 'shouting' (see p. 31).

✔ Try not to use acronyms too much. They may be
understood by your colleagues, but meaningless
to other people. If they're essential or completely
unavoidable, explain what they mean at the outset of
your message so that your correspondent can work
out what's going on.

Step four: Use an appropriate style

Clearly, there's no single style for e-mail that you can adopt
every time you compose one. You could use an informal,
chatty style when you're contacting a colleague or friend, but
it's more approriate to adopt a more formal style when
you're contacting someone for the first time or dealing with a
customer or an external contact.

✔ For colleagues or regular, familiar contacts, you could
open with 'Hi', 'Hello', or just a name ('John' or 'Sarah').
In more formal e-mails, you would use 'Dear Mr/Mrs/
Miss/Ms . . . ', or 'Dear John/Dear Sarah' if you're on
first name terms with the recipient.

TOP TIP
**Be careful about using irony in e-mails
to people who don't know you well. If
misunderstood, it could cause conflict.**

At the close of the e-mail, tailor your sign-off to your
relationship with the recipient.

Different ways of signing off

Informal

- Cheers
- Thanks
- Thx
- Ta
- All the best
- Later
- See you

More formal

- Best
- Best wishes
- All best
- All best wishes
- Many thanks
- Regards
- Kind regards
- Best regards

Very formal

- Yours ever
- Yours sincerely (if you know the name of the recipient)
- Yours faithfully (if you don't know the recipient's name and have addressed your message to 'Dear Sir or Madam')

TOP TIP
E-mail styles, like all other forms of
communication, will differ from country to
country. If you have lots of international
correspondents, remember that some
cultures are naturally more formal than
others, so take a lead from the messages
your contacts send to you and 'mirror' their
tone and style. This will mean that you're
less likely to offend anyone inadvertently.

Step five: Request the action or information you need

Some of your e-mails give information to the recipient while others make a request for action or information.

✔ If you need to find something out from somewhere, make sure you've phrased your request clearly so that they know exactly what you want. For example:

> Please could you send me the latest sales report by 22 November?

or

> Please discuss this with Tim, Omar, and Emma and let me have your views by 2.00 on Thursday.

✔ If a number of people are involved in a joint process, you may need to give them individual instructions so that everyone understands their wider role. For example:

> For the team to deliver the new product by July, we need to meet the following targets:
>
> Justin—complete the software by March
> Helen—get the test results by May
> Seema—request additional funding from the Finance Director by April

Step six: Explain how urgent your message is

✔ Make clear whether your e-mail is urgent, important, or routine. With so much e-mail traffic, people need to prioritise their reading and response, so state the level of urgency.

Some e-mail packages allow you to highlight the level of priority, but if you do use this facility, don't abuse it. It's easy to mark every e-mail as urgent or as highly important in the hope that it'll receive attention, but if you do it too often, it'll have a 'crying wolf' effect: people will start to disregard messages that you mark as urgent, even if one of them actually is. Use the facility carefully (and honestly) and you'll get the results you need.

✔ Don't use too many capital letters to indicate urgency and importance. E-mails like this can prove difficult to read on screen and, again, recipients can become immune to the technique. Also, the use of capital letters in e-mails is regarded by some people as 'virtual shouting' and your correspondents may misread your mood and respond in kind.

TOP TIP
To overcome possible reader inertia,
include an indicator in the e-mail
subject line such as 'product review–

---

decision needed by Thursday'. This is informative and gives the recipient a clear instruction.

Step seven: Use attachments to provide detail

E-mails that include longer documents, photographs, audio, or video take the form of a message plus an 'attachment'. Attachments allow you to send detailed information to your correspondent, but you should use this facility with caution.

Some attachments can take a great deal of time to transfer and the recipient may have problems downloading the attachment, particularly if they don't have broadband (which allows fast transmission of large amounts of data). Bear this in mind if you have suppliers who have small businesses or who work from home.

Attachments that could pose difficulties include:

- video clips
- publications converted to portable document format (pdf)
- presentations
- spreadsheets
- photographs

✔ Before you send attachments, check with your
correspondents that their systems can handle these
types of files.

Step eight: Include further contact details

Some e-mail programs allow you to include a 'signature' at
the end of your messages. In some cases, this can be a
scanned version of your signature, but mostly it's a few
lines that allow you to show information that the recipient
may not always have easily to hand, such as your job title,
postal address, telephone and fax number, and website
address. Adding a 'signature' is particularly useful if you're
writing to someone for the first time, as it provides some
extra context about what you do or who you work for.

TOP TIP
**Use 'signatures' to advertise a new product.
You can draw your correspondents'
attention to it by mentioning where they
can find out more about it on your website.**

Common mistakes

✗ You let your standards drop
E-mail is an instant medium, so it's easy to create a
message quickly without considering the impact on

the recipient. Abbreviations, acronyms, minimal punctuation, and unchecked spelling save time in the short term, but poor standards can damage a company's reputation.

✗ Your messages are hard to read

E-mails are normally read on a computer screen, so any information must be concise and clearly laid out. Use upper and lower case letters and a legible typeface for clarity and avoid using capital letters too much. If you have a long message, guide the recipient by using headings for different topics.

STEPS TO SUCCESS

✔ Help the recipient to prioritise the messages in his or her inbox by including a useful subject line.

✔ Make sure your e-mail is concise and mention the important points in the first few lines. Use headings to structure long passages of information.

✔ Check your spelling carefully and avoid using text message abbreviations or acronyms as much as possible.

✔ Always use good grammar and punctuation.

✔ Tailor your style to your recipient. If in doubt, take the lead from messages they send you.

✔ Give clear instructions if you need the recipient to provide information or take action.

✔ Indicate your e-mail's level of priority, but don't overuse the term 'urgent'.

✔ Use attachments to send detailed information, but make sure your recipient can download the attachments easily.

Useful links

Lancaster University Information Systems Services:
www.lancs.ac.uk/iss/email/nettiquette.htm
Netiquette home page:
www.albion.com/netiquette
Office Survival, CC Consulting:
www.crazycolour.com/os/emailedge_02.shtml

Negotiating by e-mail

Many negotiations in business today are conducted via e-mail, a process which has both advantages and disadvantages and needs careful handling to get it right.

The speed of Internet communication means that we can sometimes resolve issues more quickly than we might have done when face-to-face meetings were the only way forward. E-mail also allows us to contact people all over the world with relative ease, so rather than having to pick our way through erratic phone connections and time zones, we can send a message in the reasonable hope that the right person will get it.

However, 'virtual' negotiation misses out on many of the subtleties of negotiation we take for granted in a face-to-face meeting. When we negotiate in this way, a lot can be conveyed by our tone of voice, body language, and facial expressions. Therefore, the e-mails you use in this context need to work quite hard to get the same results. This chapter sets out to equip you with the basics that will help you succeed despite the disadvantages of 'virtual' negotiation.

Step one: Remind yourself about the principles of negotiation

Whether you negotiate face-to-face, over the phone, or by e-mail, the overall principles do not change. In basic terms, negotiation is a process with the aim of finding a balance between the objectives of two or more parties.

Before and during a negotiation:

■ prepare well. Make sure you have all the facts to hand and have read any related correspondence so you're completely up to date with the situation. Keep (and print out if you need to) all previous e-mails relevant to the negotiation in case you need to refer to them if any queries arise.

■ be sure of your own objectives. Work out your ideal scenario, a realistic scenario (that is, one that is not ideal but with which you'd still be pleased), a fallback position (that is, one that is some way removed from the ideal scenario, but which still offers something of value), and an absolute minimum resolution.

■ be clear and request clarification from others. Try to convey exactly what your position is and avoid words such as 'approximately' or 'about' so that there's absolutely no room for confusion. Similarly, if you feel unsure about what the other party is offering you, ask them to explain again.

- be prepared to be flexible. If you expect others to compromise, you need to be ready to compromise yourself.
- summarise as appropriate so that everyone is clear about what has been agreed and what further action is required (if any).

Step two: Compose the opening offer

✔ If you or your party are making the first move in the negotiation, begin by sending an e-mail to explore what the other party's expectations and ideal outcomes may be. Once you know those, and what your ideal response would be, write a well-structured e-mail that sets out:

- your offer
- prices/discounts where appropriate
- deadlines where appropriate
- any issues that are non-negotiable for legal reasons

✔ To make the e-mail easier to read, make each of these points a separate heading and use a bold font to make them stand out even more. You could also use asterisks as bullet points (your recipient may not have the capability of reading highly formatted messages, so avoid trying anything too fancy). Also avoid italics if you can as some people find them hard to read, especially on-screen.

Step three: Manage the correspondence

In some cases, an e-mail negotiation can be a simple process, involving one party making the opening offer and the other party agreeing immediately to the suggested terms. In other cases, it may be more protracted if each party has queries on the other's position or requests.

If you find yourself in this situation, you need to manage the correspondence well to keep the negotiation on track and reach a resolution that works for everyone. For example, let's look at how a customer complaint may progress through a company:

- The first e-mail from the customer sets out his or her complaint.
- In your initial reply, you acknowledge the complaint and either offer an explanation or an apology, or advise the customer that you want to investigate further.
- If you're investigating further, give the customer an approximate date for your detailed reply.
- In your detailed reply, give a full explanation and tell the customer what you're offering by way of apology or compensation.
- If the customer does not accept the explanation or the offer, you may have to take the negotiations further.
- If necessary, you can e-mail copies of all correspondence to a colleague or someone else who may be able to resolve the situation.

TOP TIP
Throughout the process, keep copies of all
e-mails so that you can refer to earlier
correspondence if circumstances
change. However, it is not necessary
to include all the previous
correspondence in each e-mail you
send — this is known as the 'thread'
and can become unwieldy.

Step four: Keep your cool

Sometimes, tempers fray during negotiations. The discussions may take longer than planned, unexpected problems may have arisen, and energy levels (as well as patience) can flag. Under these circumstances it's important to keep calm, otherwise you risk jeopardising the whole negotiation process.

✔ Adopt a polite but firm tone in all formal communications, particularly during negotiations, even if you have to deal with difficult or angry customers. It is all too easy to reply hastily to an angry message and communicate information that you may regret later.

✔ If you're angry about something, wait before replying. This will give you time to cool down and also to re-read what was actually sent to you: in the heat of the moment, you may have misread the message.

TOP TIP

If you're replying to a badly written or unclear
e-mail, maintain your own high standards
and be sure that your message is polite
and has no spelling or punctuation errors.
As a rule of thumb, make sure that any
e-mails you send as part of a negotiation
are ones that you wouldn't be ashamed
to show to your manager.

✔ If the incoming message is unclear, don't be afraid to ask
the sender for clarification. It's better to be 100% sure of
your grasp of the situation than to embark on a
protracted correspondence that will come undone at the
last minute when a major misunderstanding comes to
light. A simple 'please could you explain . . . in more
detail' should sort out any uncertainties.

TOP TIP

As in face-to-face negotiations, some people
are easier to deal with than others. If you
receive e-mails that are persistently rude
or angry from the same source, you need
to address the problem. Don't stoop to
their level and escalate the situation by
adopting the same tone: this is known as
'flaming' and is strongly discouraged in
e-mail etiquette. Instead, use polite but
assertive language to make clear that

**rudeness is unacceptable, such as
'I understand your concerns but I
believe that we can resolve the matter
more easily if we communicate calmly'.**

Step five: Watch your tone

As described above, e-mail negotiations can founder
because the correspondents miss vital clues that they
would normally pick up in face-to-face or even telephone
discussions by being able to see body language and hear
the tone of voice being used. While you're negotiating
by e-mail, think carefully about *what* you say and *how* you
say it.

TOP TIP
**If you're writing a particularly tricky or
delicate message, write a draft first, do
something else for half an hour and then
come back to it. You could ask a
trusted colleague for a second
opinion before sending it.**

Although your correspondents can't hear what you're
saying, they can certainly pick up an impression of your
mood by what you write. In your messages, try to avoid
words such as 'petty', 'trivial', 'quibbling', and 'stalling'.
Even if you think the opposite party is doing some (or
all!) of these things, you won't be helping by emphasising
this or using negative words.

TOP TIP
**Don't use capital letters or multiple
exclamation marks to emphasise a point.
Even if what you're saying isn't aggressive or
inflammatory, the way your message looks
(especially at a quick first glance) may
confuse or antagonise your correspondent.**

Step six: Summarise and conclude

An important stage in any negotiation is a summary
when the negotiations are over and agreement has been
reached. This gives everyone an opportunity to review
the decisions and to be sure that they're happy with them.

Circulating a summary by e-mail is fine, especially for
internal negotiations, but you may want to follow up by
letter if you've been dealing with an external client.
Remember to be clear and concise in your summary, using
headings and bullet points as appropriate.

TOP TIP
**Try to write your summary as soon as you
can after the negotiation has been
concluded so that you can easily
remember all the decisions. The
longer you leave it, the more
painful a process it will be!**

Common mistakes

✗ **You don't take enough care composing your messages**

Time is at a premium for all of us, but it's well worth spending as much time as you can over your messages when you're negotiating by e-mail. Whether you're composing your initial offer or trying to seal the deal, check over your message before you send it to make sure that it's completely clear, polite, and has no spelling mistakes. If you have some spare time, leave your message for a few minutes and then come back to it—you're bound to spot something you've missed.

✗ **You send a message you regret**

If you lose your temper while you're negotiating and fire off an e-mail that makes your mood very clear to your recipient, you've some work to do. Apologise as quickly as you can (it's probably best to do this by telephone) and try to establish a co-operative atmosphere again. You can do this by recapping what you've agreed on, as this will remind the other party that you're not always unreasonable!

STEPS TO SUCCESS

✔ Spend as much time as you need in preparation before negotiating. It's never wasted time.

✔ Make sure you're aware of all relevant facts.

✔ If your party is making the opening offer, write a simple, clearly-structured e-mail setting out your position.

✔ Ask for clarification if you need it when you receive the counter-offer.

✔ If your correspondent becomes aggressive, don't reply in anger. Draft a reply and cool down before you send it.

✔ Remember that e-mail negotiation can't rely on the visual or physical 'clues' that face-to-face negotiation can, so be careful not to use language that will annoy the other party.

✔ Summarise and conclude by letter if appropriate.

Useful links

'Email and the Schmooze Factor', Stanford GSB:
**www.gsb.stanford.edu/research/reports/1999/
morris.html**
Emailreplies.com:
www.emailreplies.com
'How to Avoid the Pitfalls of Negotiating over Email',
Watershed Associates:
**www.watershedassociates.com/pdf/Watershed%
20on%20Email%20Negotiations%20TW.pdf**

Dealing with difficult e-mail situations

The immediacy with which e-mail allows us to communicate with others is both one of its great advantages and one of its disadvantages. Sometimes, especially when time is short, people feel under pressure to reply to e-mails as soon as they land in their inbox and this can cause all sorts of problems.

This chapter sets out to offer advice on what to do if you find yourself in a difficult situation that has been caused or made worse by e-mail, including sending an e-mail to the wrong person and replying in haste or anger.

Step one: Make sure you read your messages properly

Stating the obvious? Not for some harassed people. If you have lots of demands on your time, it's all too easy to misread e-mails, especially if they're badly written or unclear in tone or layout. While replying promptly to messages of any kind is something we all aim for, beware of writing back too quickly if you're not 100% sure of what your correspondent is requesting or writing about.

✔ Use the staged approach outlined in Chapter 2 to acknowledge receipt of an e-mail, request clarification if you need it, and reply fully when you're up to speed with all the relevant information.

Step two: Check you're replying to the right person

If you're involved in an exchange of e-mails between a group of people, take great care when you reply.

✔ If you're annoyed or exasperated by a group e-mail, resist at all costs the temptation to write while you're still angry. Give yourself some cooling-off time first. If you do choose to reply, only reply to the group if it's absolutely necessary and if you reply to just one person, make doubly-sure before you send the e-mail that the addressee is the right person! For example, some of your correspondents may have similar first or surnames, so check before you click 'send'.

TOP TIP

Also take care if you're replying to personal e-mails at work. There are always horror stories in the newspapers about people who think they're writing to friends or partners but who inadvertently send highly personal messages to everyone

---

in their address book or click on just 'reply to
sender'. This not only causes acute (and
very public!) embarrassment, but also
puts the writer in the firing line back at
the office. Always take time to check,
but better still, send personal e-mails
from a non-work e-mail account.

Step three: Be careful when you forward information to other people

✔ In the same way that you need to take care when
originating or replying to an e-mail, watch your step
when you forward information on to another person,
especially if he or she is an external client or customer.
As mentioned above, double-check you're sending the
e-mail to the right person and haven't accidentally
clicked 'reply' instead of 'forward'.

In some cases, where the 'thread' of e-mail conversation
is quite long or you've only been copied in for some part
of it, you might not realise if some of the comments or
content interleaved isn't appropriate for passing on. These
comments could range from the relatively harmless ('I hope
we tie this up soon: the negotiation's gone on for longer
than I'd hoped') to the disastrous ('I hope we never have to
work with these people again').

TOP TIP

Make sure you aren't passing on anything that comments unfavourably on the external party's capabilities or judgment. Also double-check that there are no personal, offensive, or defamatory remarks (such as any that criticise appearance, are racist, or sexist).

Step four: Treat confidential information carefully

E-mails have been described as electronic postcards—their contents can be easily read by anyone—so make sure you read through external e-mails before you send them to make sure you haven't inadvertently included confidential or sensitive information.

If you do need to send confidential information to a correspondent, you can include it in your e-mail as a password-protected attachment.

TOP TIP

Check your company's policy on confidentiality and security. It should set out what can and cannot be sent by e-mail. It will also set out the disclaimers or warnings that should be included in every e-mail.

Step five: Deal immediately with e-mails sent in error

Despite your best efforts and the advice above, sometimes (especially if you have an extensive mailing list) you may write or send something to the wrong person. In many cases, this may be perfectly harmless, but, if the information is confidential or critical of the unintended recipient or their company, you may have a problem.

Many companies put a disclaimer on all outgoing e-mails saying that the information they contain is intended for the recipient only. The disclaimer might also say that the information is confidential. Even with these disclaimers, though, the damage is done as soon as the e-mail has been sent so you need to act quickly.

✔ If you've sent a potentially damaging e-mail by mistake, contact the recipient as quickly as possible, either by phone or by e-mail.

TOP TIP

Some e-mail programs allow you to recall sent messages. However, this will normally depend upon the recipient using the same e-mail program as you, being logged on at the time, but not having read the message at the time you wish to recall it. So don't rely on this option!

✔ If the material is confidential, ask the recipient to destroy it securely, if possible.

✔ Apologise if the material contains critical or offensive remarks and offer an explanation.

✔ If you can, try to speak to your manager as soon as you can so that they're prepared in case the other party wishes to make a complaint. You may find this embarrassing, but in the long run it will save time and help to put a 'cap' on the situation.

TOP TIP

If you find yourself in a position like this, it's important to be polite but fair. Your aim is to resolve the situation as quickly as possible, with minimal damage and inconvenience. Don't be sarcastic, try to make too much of a joke of it (jokes often don't travel well online), or be rude. If you feel that things are escalating beyond your control, talk to your boss, explaining exactly what happened and when.

Step six: Don't involve other people unnecessarily in an argument

'War by memo' has now evolved to 'war by e-mail'. The practice of sending copies of communications to as many

---

people as possible in order to impress or embarrass is much simpler with e-mail but is a waste of time, energy, and inbox space.

If you have a problem with a colleague or external client, write to them directly. (Telephoning them may actually be the best way to reach a solution as the voice can convey nuances that e-mail will never be able to.) There's no need to copy in everyone in your team unless there is an essential business reason for you to do so.

Common mistakes

✗ You scan your e-mails rather than reading them properly before you reply

If you receive a large number of e-mails daily and are under time pressure, you might think you're saving time by scanning the messages for key words and then replying. In some cases this will be fine, but in others it will set you off on the wrong foot. Don't reply in a rush, especially if it's an important message: send an acknowledgment and write back properly when you've more time to dedicate to writing a great e-mail.

✗ You allow a difficult situation to escalate

If you receive an angry or rude e-mail, it can be tempting to reply in the same tone, but this will just make things worse. Keep cool, act professionally, and reply in measured language. If you feel that you've been rude already and have some ground to make up, apologise to your correspondent.

STEPS TO SUCCESS

✔ Always be fair and polite in your e-mails, even if people are rude to you.

✔ Keep the number of people on your distribution list to a minimum.

✔ Avoid sending personal e-mails from your work address.

✔ Check your message is addressed to the right person!

✔ Take immediate action to deal with any e-mails that you've sent in error and be ready to apologise.

✔ Check that any message you're forwarding doesn't contain inappropriate comments in the thread.

✔ Familiarise yourself with your company's confidentiality and security policies.

Useful links

'8 e-mail mistakes that make you look bad', bcentral.co.uk:
**www.bcentral.co.uk/technology/networks/
8mistakes.asp**

'A Beginner's Guide to Effective Email', webfoot.com:

www.webfoot.com/advice/email.top.html

Emailreplies.com:

www.emailreplies.com

Emailtools.co.uk:

www.emailtools.co.uk/tips/topmistakes.htm

Tiger Computing Ltd:

www.tiger-computing.co.uk/email.pdf

'Top 10 email mistakes', ibiztips.com:

www.ibiztips.com/email31AUG00.htm and

www.ibiztips.com/email04SEP00.htm

Using e-mail with other forms of communication

E-mail is a powerful medium in its own right, but it can also be used to enhance other forms of communication. Sometimes, e-mail may not be the most effective approach, so you need to consider whether a telephone call or a conventional letter might be more appropriate.

A telephone call may be preferable to sending an e-mail for example, if you need to have a two-way discussion with someone. But you can use e-mail to exchange background information and summarise the outcome of your discussion. Write a letter if you wish to include confidential information or if you're covering a formal topic and you want to ensure that the recipient has a printed copy of the information you're sending.

Another important area in which you should consider using e-mail is your company website. Including e-mail facilities within the website makes it easier for site visitors to contact you or request additional information. Make sure that you always include an e-mail address at the end of your company advertising. When customers contact you, you can capture their details and open up a sales process.

If you send direct mail to customers, you can use e-mail to follow-up the mailing and improve the effectiveness of the campaign. For example, your company may use telemarketing to contact customers or sales prospects initially and then follow up with e-mail.

Step one: Use telephone and e-mail together for detailed discussions

Although e-mail is a very quick, effective method of communicating information, it may not always be the most appropriate medium if you need to have a detailed discussion with someone. In this situation, using the telephone may be more suitable. You can, however, use e-mail *in conjunction with* the telephone to help you have a more effective discussion.

✔ If you want to hold a detailed discussion with one or more people, e-mail them in advance to outline the key points you wish to discuss and arrange a convenient time for the call. This gives the other parties time to prepare and gather information so that they can make a useful contribution to the discussion. It also gives them the opportunity to make some space in their schedule when they can speak to you without interruption.

✔ During the telephone call, you can e-mail information that might help the discussion along—a set of figures, a diagram, or other material that would be difficult to describe by phone.

✔ After the discussion, you can send an e-mail summarising the main conclusions and action points from the discussion. Alternatively, if you're using a voice-conferencing service, you can ask the service provider to record the call and e-mail participants an electronic copy of the discussion as an attachment. This facility is particularly useful for confirming the points of long, complicated discussions.

Step two: Send a letter as well as an e-mail for more formal communications

For certain types of formal correspondence, such as commercial agreements, appointments and dismissals, confirmation of contracts, and other material which might be legally binding, you may find it more appropriate to send a conventional letter. Although techniques such as digital signatures have given e-mail increased status as legal documents, a printed letter with a handwritten signature continues to carry greater weight in law.

The problem with conventional letters, however, is that they take longer to reach the recipient, so where time is critical, you could send an advance copy of a letter by e-mail.

Step three: Include e-mail facilities within your website

Websites are a proven, cost-effective method of giving visitors access to large amounts of complex company and product information. However, if a website includes no facilities for communication, those resources can be wasted.

E-mail opens up a channel of communication that can turn browsers into buyers. Each site should include a 'Contact us' page or section that displays the company address, telephone, and fax details. It should also include an e-mail address such as sales@abc.com, info@abc.com, or feedback@abc.com.

✔ Adding an electronic form to your site that encourages visitors to register their details can prove even more valuable. Don't make the mistake of asking visitors for too many details as this will irritate them, but ask for some basic ones, including their e-mail address. Once you have this, you can give them the option of being e-mailed with details of products that might be of interest or special offers (you must get their permission to do this first!). This will create valuable sales leads which the sales force can follow up.

TOP TIP

**Give visitors the option of subscribing to
e-mail alerts. Here visitors register their
interest in particular products or services
and receive a personalised e-mail
whenever there is a new development.**

Step four: Include an e-mail address on your advertisements

If your company uses advertising to promote products and
services, you can increase the return on your expenditure
by including an e-mail address in the advertisement.
The e-mail address encourages readers to respond by
requesting further information. This is known as 'direct
response advertising'.

Some advertisements include postal addresses or
telephone numbers as a 'response mechanism'. E-mail has
an advantage over these mechanisms because it's quick
and easy to use. Remember that advertisers have to
overcome a high inertia factor, so employ the simplest
technique possible.

✔ Including an e-mail address on advertisements also
   enables you to measure the effectiveness of your
   campaign in terms of the number of responses. You can
   measure overall responses or compare the performance

of different media by using a different e-mail address on each publication such as info1@abc.com or infotv@abc.com.

Step five: Use e-mail in conjunction with direct mail

Some companies send information to customers and prospects via conventional mail. This is known as direct mail and it's used as an alternative to advertising to communicate with smaller or more specialised groups of customers and sales prospects.

✔ Use e-mail to increase the effectiveness of direct mail campaigns. By sending a 'teaser' e-mail, you can encourage the audience to watch out for the main mailing. (Remember that by law, you must gain your correspondents' prior permission, though.) For example:

> In just over a week, you'll find out how you could save your company thousands of pounds.

✔ After the direct mail has been sent out, follow up:

> We hope you received details of our great special offer. Don't forget to reply by 10 November to qualify for a massive discount.

Once a prospective customer has responded, e-mail them regularly with updates.

Step six: Improve telemarketing with e-mail

Telemarketing is the use of the telephone to carry out market research or to sell products and services to customers and prospects. Telemarketing is proving to be more effective when it's used with other media. For example, if you or your staff are responsible for making calls of this kind, you can send, as e-mail attachments, product information such as data, diagrams, or other illustrations that help the prospective buyer to understand what you're offering.

TOP TIP
**After making a telemarketing call, send an
e-mail thanking the customer for their time
and confirming any product, price, or delivery
details that have been discussed or agreed.**

Step seven: Set up an e-mail forum for customers

An Internet forum is a discussion group for people with similar interests. In business, it's increasingly used to build stronger relationships with customers.

As an example, a technology company could set up a forum where customers are able to exchange technical information with each other and discuss questions of mutual interest. The forum could also be used to resolve problems that a number of different customers experience.

✔ E-mail is an ideal medium for forum discussions. The company that hosts the forum sets up an e-mail facility on its website and manages the process. E-mails are posted on a notice board and members can contribute to any relevant discussions.

Common mistakes

✗ **You use e-mail in the wrong circumstances**
E-mail is seen as a communications tool suitable for all situations. There are, however, some occasions when a letter or telephone call may be more appropriate. Assess the circumstances and make sure you're using the right method at the right time.

✗ **You don't recognise the contribution e-mail can make to other communications**
E-mail can also be used to support your sales and marketing processes. By using e-mail as part of advertising, websites, direct mail, and telemarketing campaigns, you can make your marketing budget go further and get great results.

✗ **You alienate potential customers with sloppy e-mail marketing**
Never e-mail someone without their permission, send

them irrelevant information, or over-e-mail them. Impress customers with well-written, thoroughly proof-read e-mails, and always give them the option to 'unsubscribe'.

STEPS TO SUCCESS

✔ Make a telephone call when you need to have detailed discussions with someone, but use e-mail to make the call more effective by sending useful attachments for reference during the conversation, and by summarising any decisions reached.

✔ Send a letter when you need to confirm information that is legally binding.

✔ If your business has a website, make it easier for visitors to contact you by including e-mail contact facilities.

✔ Make advertisements work harder by giving prospective clients an e-mail address to request further information.

✔ If you have permission, use e-mail in conjunction with direct mail to achieve better results.

✔ Improve the effectiveness of telemarketing by using e-mail to send information during and after a sales call.

✔ Set up an e-mail discussion forum to strengthen relationships with customers.

Useful links

emailtools.co.uk:

www.emailtools.co.uk/tips

UK Online:

www.ukonlineforbusiness.gov.uk

Carrying out special e-mail tasks

E-mail is now the established medium for routine business communications, but it also has a number of important specialist tasks that can be used to improve productivity and understanding inside and outside a company.

E-mail can be used in two apparently conflicting ways. It's ideal for broadcasting information to a large group of people quickly and cost-effectively, but can also be used to send personalised information to individuals or small sections within the larger group.

Because e-mail is simple and widely used, it can speed up a number of important business processes. For example, you can set up automated facilities to deal with requests for information, service queries, or other routine requests. It's also ideal for managing the high volume of regular communications for particular groups of employees such as sales representatives or members of a project team.

This chapter also shows how e-mail, used responsibly, can be a fast, effective, and cheap marketing tool.

Step one: Distribute general interest messages

If you need to reach a large group of people with the same information, e-mail is an ideal way of doing it. For example, if you wanted to announce a new appointment or a big sales success, you could send one message to everyone in the company. That represents a huge saving in terms of the time, effort, and paper needed to distribute printed information to the same group of people.

Useful items to announce include:

- trading results
- company policy changes
- organisational changes or new appointments
- sales successes
- personnel issues

TOP TIP
Remember to use 'broadcast mailings' sensibly. Try not to send messages that are of little interest or importance to the majority of employees—only pass on information with genuine news value. Some companies appoint one person as an 'arbiter' of this type of e-mail, and anyone who wants to send one has to ask that person before sending the message.

Step two: Set up special interest groups

As well as simplifying mass communication, e-mail is also a great way of keeping in contact with groups of people such as customers, colleagues, retailers, journalists, investors, or other groups with an interest in different aspects of your company. Because e-mail is a low-cost way of sending and receiving information, you can sub-divide each group further and send personalised information to small groups. For example, you could divide customers into categories such as:

- small, medium, or large businesses
- existing customers or prospective customers
- companies in different industries
- partners

Companies or individuals who receive targeted information like this generally think it more valuable than large amounts of general information that may be irrelevant.

TOP TIP
Take the process of targeting further by asking recipients to specify the type of information they'd like to receive from you and how frequently they'd like to receive it. This eliminates waste and guarantees a high level of interest in information that you distribute.

Step three: Produce an electronic newsletter

An electronic newsletter can be used to communicate regularly and cost-effectively with either large groups or special interest groups. Newsletters can contain a selection of articles of interest to the audience and can be published daily, weekly, monthly, or at a frequency determined by the amount of new information.

✔ Although theoretically there is no limit to the amount of information that can be included in an electronic newsletter, one that is too long may prove difficult to read on a computer screen. To get around this problem, include summaries of the articles within the newsletter and if readers want to read more, they can click on a hyperlink that takes them to a more detailed version held on a website or an e-mail server.

✔ To make the newsletter more valuable, ask readers to subscribe by providing details of their interest or by paying an appropriate fee. Requesting subscriber information is also a useful way of personalising the newsletter and ensuring that it contains information of real interest to the reader.

✔ As with all formal e-mails, make sure that the newsletter is thoroughly checked for spelling and grammar. Also include the option to 'unsubscribe' at the end of each newsletter.

Step four: Simplify requests for information

Many of the requests for information that a company receives are simple and easy to handle (queries about prices, availability, or requests for brochures, for example). However, companies have to allocate staff to handle these inquiries by telephone and this can prove time-consuming.

Setting up an e-mail facility simplifies the process and can save a company time and money.

✔ Ask your IT helpdesk to set up a facility that carries an e-mail address such as information@abccompany.com or sales@abccompany.com. Several e-mail addresses could be offered to help filter the type of request and make sure it gets to the right person. You could have e-mail addresses for different products or departments, for example.

When someone sends a request, such as 'please send me a brochure' or 'ask a sales representative to contact me', there should be an automated response. This can take the form of a short message such as 'Thank you for your request. We will respond to you within 24 hours'. Staff can then deal with the request at a convenient time so long as it is within the agreed timescale. If they need more information from the person who sent the request, they can use e-mail to ask questions.

Step five: Set up an online self-service facility

✔ Use the same principle to help customers request service assistance or resolve straightforward problems themselves. This facility would carry an address such as service@abccompany.com. Customers could place a request such as 'please ask a service engineer to call to repair my machine'. The company could then allocate a time and confirm the appointment by return.

Alternatively, the customer could describe the problem in the e-mail. The company then has a choice of e-mailing a reply to the customer, phoning to discuss the problem, or dispatching an engineer for an urgent or serious problem. The facility could also be linked to a series of frequently-asked questions (FAQs). When the customer sends the first e-mail, the reply could include a link to the FAQs, enabling the customers to solve many simple problems themselves quickly and easily.

TOP TIP
Techniques like this can save a company considerable time in dealing with routine service issues. That, in turn, frees support staff to concentrate on more complex or urgent customer problems.

Step six: Run a project by e-mail

Projects, such as marketing campaigns, new product development programmes, or company re-organisation, generate high levels of information and communication that can be handled effectively by e-mail. E-mail gives every member of a project team access to the same information, wherever they are, making it simple for people in different locations to work together without constantly travelling to meetings.

Project communications would include:

- inter-team messages
- project updates
- budget reports
- scheduling changes
- requests for information
- status reports
- minutes of meetings
- action lists
- problems to be resolved
- sources of information

By using e-mail in conjunction with a technique such as videoconferencing or teleconferencing, communications can become even more sophisticated. As an example, a meeting that involved people from five different sites could be held by teleconference, eliminating unnecessary travelling and enabling meetings to be set up at short notice. Many teleconferencing services include facilities for recording the entire meeting. The recording can be distributed immediately to all participants as an e-mail attachment.

Step seven: Set up a sales force communication channel

Sales representatives are one group of staff who spend a lot of time away from the office, yet they need a great deal of up-to-date information to do their job well.

E-mail is an ideal tool for distributing important sales information and maintaining communications with people who are constantly on the move. It can be used for updates such as:

- price changes
- product information
- customer records
- new orders
- late payments
- customer problems
- delivery details

The sales force can also use e-mail to request information or to send reports and other customer information to the office. Like the online service facilities described earlier in the chapter, many of these processes can be automated to speed up and simplify communications.

Common mistakes

✗ You mass-mail irrelevant information

E-mail can be used to send the same information to large numbers of people. This is only valuable if the information is relevant to all the people on the mailing list. It may be more appropriate to mail selectively.

✗ You start to rely too heavily on automated e-mail facilities

Automated facilities are a great way to handle incoming requests for service or information. However, if they're not backed up by effective customer service, they can damage a company's reputation. An immediate automated response that tells a customer you've received their request is pointless if the customer then has to wait weeks for the information.

✗ Your e-mails aren't personalised

E-mail can be easily personalised and including information that a recipient actually wants ensures that it will be read and acted on rather than left to languish in someone's inbox.

STEPS TO SUCCESS

✓ Use e-mail to reach large groups of people quickly and cost-effectively.

✔ Personalise e-mail to ensure that it only contains information that is relevant to special interest groups.

✔ Create electronic newsletters to communicate more detailed information in a convenient, easy-to-read format.

✔ Set up automated e-mail facilities to simplify the handling of routine requests for information or service.

✔ Provide self-service facilities for customers using e-mail as the first point of contact.

✔ Improve the productivity of project groups by making full use of e-mail for team communications.

✔ Use e-mail and automated e-mail facilities to help sales representatives and other staff working away from the office to access information quickly and easily.

Useful links

Business Know-how:
www.businessknowhow.com
UK Online:
www.ukonlineforbusiness.gov.uk

Using e-mail responsibly

While e-mail can really help you improve your performance at work, it can also put you and your company at risk. An e-mail may have the same legal status as a letter, so if you inadvertently harm someone's reputation, cause offence, or spread a computer virus, you could face disciplinary action or even legal charges.

Fortunately, most companies recognise the risks inherent in e-mail and publish guidelines on acceptable usage. Others may monitor incoming and outgoing e-mails to prevent and control the level of risk. Practices like this have raised complex privacy and legal issues which currently contain many grey areas. As with most work-related issues, it's important to be sensible and be aware of your responsibilities.

Step one: Keep personal e-mail to a minimum

Industry experience indicates that more than 50% of e-mails going through company systems are for personal use. While individual employees find this valuable, companies believe that it can slow down urgent business e-mails, reduce productivity, and increase the risk of viruses being introduced into the system. As a result, many organisations have introduced guidelines on personal use of e-mail at work.

✔ Check to see if your company has any guidelines on this issue. Remember that even though your employer may not mind the occasional use of e-mail for personal messages, he or she will soon get fed up if it looks as if staff are taking advantage. If you do make some personal use of your work e-mail, don't abuse it.

TOP TIP

Keep personal messages sent from your work account short and few in number, and don't send unacceptable content—you could face disciplinary action. The best thing to do is to get your friends and family to contact you via an Internet-based e-mail provider such as Hotmail, Yahoo, or AOL. That way your business and personal e-mail are kept completely separate.

Step two: Recognise what is acceptable in business e-mail

Your company's guidelines should indicate what is, and what is not, 'acceptable' usage. If your company has no guidelines, use your common sense. The main areas of unacceptable usage appear to be:

- circulating malicious office gossip
- circulating pornographic content (text or images)
- harassing other employees
- circulating racist, sexist, or politically-offensive material
- circulating defamatory remarks about individuals or companies
- highlighting mistakes made by other employees

These are broad categories of content and the degree of acceptability is open to interpretation by individual companies. There have been examples in the press where, in one company, employees have been dismissed for circulating content that, in other companies, would have only incurred a warning. If you're in any doubt, ask your company to clarify what they mean by acceptable content or, in extreme cases, take legal advice.

TOP TIP

Don't use e-mail to say something that you wouldn't include in a letter. Also, if you think someone has sent you a message that contains inappropriate content of any kind, imagine what you'd do if your boss turned up just as you opened it. What would the consequences be? It's best to delete e-mails of this kind without even opening them, and then empty your 'deleted items' folder or 'wastebin'.

Step three: Understand the issue of e-mail privacy

Closely linked to the question of acceptable use is the issue of privacy. If companies issue guidelines on e-mail use, they may also operate monitoring systems to check that e-mail is being used correctly. The legal position is not entirely clear-cut here.

Some commentators believe that employers should make it clear that they monitor all e-mail for technical reasons. They feel that the 2000 Regulation of Investigatory Powers Act opened the way for widespread monitoring of staff communications including the opening of e-mails and the checking of voicemail and Internet usage.

However, other commentators feel that the 1998 Data Protection Act appeared to give some protection to employees by stating that employers should *not* open e-mails that were clearly personal. It also stated that any monitoring should be carried out in a 'fair and appropriate way'.

The Employment Practices Data Protection Code: Monitoring at Work, issued in 2003 by the Information Commissioner, is a good practice guide designed to help employers comply with the Data Protection Act, but given the 'grey areas' in interpretation of legislation, it may be worth taking professional legal advice in the event of a dispute.

Step four: Watch out for e-mail viruses

One of the main reasons companies monitor e-mail is to protect their computer systems against viruses and other security risks. There have been a number of high-profile viruses in recent years, including 'Melissa, 'Mydoom', and 'Love Bug'. They appear in an inbox as harmless-looking e-mails with attachments but, as soon as the attachments are opened, the virus starts to take effect.

Often the effect of the virus is annoying, rather than harmful, but there are a large number of viruses that can cause serious damage to a company's computer systems. To avoid the risk of virus damage, make sure that you follow the guidelines featured in chapter 2.

TOP TIP
Don't open e-mail attachments from an
unknown source. Viruses are carried
in attachments, not messages, so
opening the message itself should
not cause any problems.

Step five: Comply with company confidentiality agreements

As well as security threats from incoming e-mails, companies also recognise the risk that outgoing e-mails pose. There are a number of potential problems:

- sending confidential information to an incorrect address
- expressing opinions in the e-mail that might lead the recipient to take legal action against your company
- inadvertently including a virus that infects the recipient's system

The prime responsibility for checking the content of outgoing e-mails is yours, but many companies recommend that you also include a disclaimer at the end of your message. Here are two examples:

Disclaimer example 1

Due to the nature of the Internet, the sender is unable to ensure the integrity of this message and does not accept any liability or responsibility for any errors or omissions (whether as the result of this message having been intercepted or otherwise) in the contents of this message. Any views expressed in this communication are those of the individual sender, except where the sender specifically states them to be the views of the company.

Disclaimer example 2

The information contained in this e-mail may be subject to public disclosure under the Freedom of Information Act 2000. Unless the information is legally exempt from disclosure, the confidentiality of this e-mail and your reply cannot be guaranteed. The unauthorised use, disclosure, copying, or alteration of this message or any information contained within it is forbidden. It is intended for the addressee only. If you are not the intended recipient, please notify the sender immediately and delete the e-mail from your system. The views expressed within this e-mail are not necessarily the views or policies of THIS COMPANY. E-mails are not considered a secure medium for sending personal information and may be at risk. Recipients should run anti-virus software before opening any attachments. All liability is excluded to the extent permitted by law for any claims arising from the use of this medium by this organisation.

Step six: Store business e-mails for the required period

High-profile court cases such as Enron and Worldcom have highlighted the importance of good record keeping in business and this extends to e-mails. Companies must make sure that e-mails sent on a company's behalf are stored for a period that meets increasingly complex corporate legislation and regulatory requirements. These are just some of the requirements:

■ regulations, determined by organisations such as the Information Commissioner under the Data Protection Act, govern how long business-related e-mail has to be retained and affect how quickly it needs to be retrieved

- for companies operating internationally, compliance and regulatory requirements and timescales vary from country to country
- in the United States, there are some 10,000 regulations governing storage, availability, and disposal of different types of business data
- some industries such as finance and healthcare must have an e-mail storage strategy as a prerequisite for doing business

When courts request original documents such as financial statements, advice to investors, and internal e-mails, companies must be able to provide them with copies. Since more than 90% of documents are now created electronically, this means that copies of e-mails must be stored and archived with the same care as equivalent paper documents.

However, the actual retention periods can vary considerably, depending on the type of document, its source, and its content. The problem is that these 'predetermined periods' vary from country to country and from industry to industry. In the United States, the Securities and Exchange Commission requires records to be kept for predetermined periods, up to 7 years in some cases. In the United Kingdom, the Data Protection Act requires non-essential data to be destroyed after 2 years.

✔ The best and safest thing you can do is to find out your company's policy on storing e-mails and make sure that you comply.

TOP TIP
Set up a filing system to make sure that you
can find business e-mails quickly and easily.
Check with your company's IT helpdesk,
who should be able to let you know how
long you need to keep copies. To save
space on your server, the helpdesk will
be able to help you set up archives
that can be accessed as necessary.

Common mistakes

✗ You take advantage of the facilities at work

While it's handy to be able to make or confirm social
arrangements, moan about your boss, or gossip with
your friends using your work e-mail, remember that you're
being paid to do some work! There is bound to be some
personal use of work e-mail facilities, but try to play fair:
don't do it all the time, as if everyone else in the company
is doing it too, it's likely that the management will pick up
on it and do something drastic about it. Be sensible.

**✗ You don't understand what 'acceptable'
content is**

Linked to the point above is the concept of 'acceptable'
e-mail content. Never say anything about anyone over
e-mail that you wouldn't say in a letter, even if you're
upset, annoyed, or frustrated. You could very easily
send your message to the wrong person, which would

be embarrassing enough, but remember that messages you send can and will be kept by people who might report you to your manager if what you've written is unacceptable.

✗ You think that no one will notice what you write

Some companies have a policy of monitoring e-mails sent by their employees. The law relating to this area is so unclear at present that it's worth playing safe at all times. Just don't send e-mails that you'd be ashamed of in a few hours' or days' time.

✗ You don't know what to do about e-mail viruses

Viruses are often sent to people in the form of an e-mail plus an attachment. If you're in any doubt whatsoever about the provenance or safety of an e-mail attachment, don't open it; delete the message and then empty your 'deleted items' folder. If you're unsure of, or worried about, a message, contact your IT helpdesk (if your company has one).

STEPS TO SUCCESS

✔ Use your company e-mail system for business. Keep personal use to a minimum.

✔ Make sure you understand what constitutes acceptable e-mail content.

✔ Recognise that your company may monitor e-mails and keep private and confidential material to a minimum.

✔ Be careful about incoming e-mail; it could introduce potentially damaging viruses.

✔ Check your outgoing e-mails to make sure that you do not inadvertently release confidential material to the wrong recipient.

✔ Find out how long you have to retain business e-mails and store them safely.

Useful links

Information Commissioner's Office:
www.informationcommissioner.gov.uk
IT Week:
www.itweek.co.uk
Yourrights.org.uk:
www.yourrights.org.uk/faqs/privacy/monitoring-my-telephone-and-email.shtml

Where to find more help

Better, Faster Email: Getting the Most Out of Email
Joan Tunstall
Crows Nest, New South Wales: Allen & Unwin, 1999
192pp ISBN 1864488999
This practical introductory guide covers topics such as overcoming problems with attachments, e-mail netiquette tips, coping with an overflowing inbox, keeping a hard copy record, maintaining privacy, writing better e-mails, and sending messages quickly. Each chapter ends with a summary of the key points and some exercises to help the reader assess their skills.

Canning Spam: You've Got Mail (That You Don't Want)
Jeremy Poteet
Indianapolis, IN: Sams, 2004
320pp ISBN 0672326396
The author offers advice on how to prevent unwanted e-mails getting through to users, and what to do to avoid the spread of malicious messages if something does get through. The book explains how spammers gain access to e-mail addresses and how attackers can trick users into opening messages. Each chapter includes practical advice for administrators setting policy and installing filters to block spam, as well as tips for users to help them avoid becoming part of the problem.

Managing in the Email Office
Monica Seeley, Gerrard Hargreaves
Oxford: Butterworth-Heinemann, 2003
256pp ISBN 0750656980
Aimed at managers and those who have the freedom to organise their own working day, this guide offers help on how to manage both your own flow of e-mail as well as your organisation's. The solutions are based on preferred patterns of work and management styles, and case histories are included to support these ideas. The authors show how time management and personal effectiveness can be

improved through e-mail and how it can be used to support a knowledge management and information-sharing culture.

Managing Your E-Mail: Thinking Outside the In-Box
Christina Cavanagh
Chichester: John Wiley, 2003
208pp ISBN 0471457388
This accessible reference offers solutions for dealing with e-mail inefficiencies, practical tips on getting and staying organised, and real-life anecdotes. Its topics include prioritising and responding to e-mail, knowing when to choose more traditional communication methods, managing career-limiting e-mail temptations, how to write more impactful and readable messages, how to reduce e-mail volume, and the legal pitfalls to avoid.

Office Emails That Really Click
Maureen Chase, Sandy Trupp
Hampton, VA: Aegis Publishing Group, Ltd., 2000
224pp ISBN 1890154180
The authors have produced a useful reference tool that covers the dos and don'ts of e-mail etiquette in an accessible and witty way. The book also provides guidance on common grammar problems, spamming, viruses, toolbar functions, and privacy, and is full of clear descriptions and examples of good and bad e-mail techniques.

Total E-mail Marketing
Dave Chaffey
Oxford: Butterworth-Heinemann, 2002
228pp ISBN 0750657545
This book demonstrates how to gain new customers and get closer to existing ones by the effective planning and execution of e-mail campaigns. Packed with examples, case studies from UK companies, and checklists to get you started or improve on past campaigns, it covers topics like planning and monitoring integrated e-mail campaigns, writing great copy, building a quality house list, understanding ethical and legal constraints, and using tools for managing in- and out-bound e-mail.